The Soft Skills Power

*A New Look at Soft Skills:
How Emotional Intelligence
Can Drive IT Success*

Maxwell Rowan

© **Copyright 2023 - All rights reserved.**

The contents of this book may not be reproduced, duplicated or transmitted without direct written permission from the author.

Under no circumstances will any legal responsibility or blame be held against the publisher for any reparation, damages, or monetary loss due to the information herein, either directly or indirectly.

Legal Notice:
This book is copyright protected. This is only for personal use. You cannot amend, dis-tribute, sell, use, quote or paraphrase any part or the content within this book without the consent of the author.

Disclaimer Notice:
Please note the information contained within this document is for educational and entertainment purposes only. Every attempt has been made to provide accurate, up to date and reliable complete information. Readers acknowledge that the author is not engaging in the rendering of legal, financial, medical or professional advice. The content of this book has been derived from various sources. Please consult a licensed professional before attempting any techniques outlined in this book.

By reading this document, the reader agrees that under no circumstances is the author responsible for any losses, direct or indirect, which are incurred as a result of the use of information contained within this document.

Table of Contents

Introduction 5

Chapter One: Understanding Soft Skills................................ 8

Chapter Two: Emotional Intelligence 16

Chapter Three: Communication 24

Chapter Four: Collaboration and Teamwork........................ 32

Chapter Five: Leadership and Management........................40

Chapter Six: Conflict Resolution..48

Chapter Seven: Work-Life Balance and Well-Being............... 55

Chapter Eight: Creativity and Innovation in Tech.................. 62

Chapter Nine: Diversity and Inclusion in Tech 69

Conclusions..77

Introduction

In today's world, technology plays an increasingly significant role in virtually every aspect of our lives. From the devices we use to stay connected to the software that powers our workplaces, it's hard to overstate the importance of technology in the 21st century.

And yet, despite this ever-growing reliance on technology, there's a critical component of success in the tech industry that's all too often overlooked: soft skills. These intangible qualities that help individuals connect with others, work collaboratively, and navigate complex social dynamics are often seen as less important than the "hard skills" of programming, data analysis, and technical expertise.

But the truth is that soft skills are every bit as important in the tech industry as they are in any other field. In fact, one could argue that they are even more essential in a world where technology is constantly evolving and the pace of change is faster than ever before.

So why are soft skills so often overlooked in the tech industry? There are a number of reasons, ranging from cultural factors to simple ignorance.

One major factor is the stereotype of the "tech genius" - the idea that the most successful tech professionals are those who possess a natural talent for coding and other technical skills. This stereotype can create a culture in which soft skills are undervalued and even stigmatized.

Another factor is the tendency to view technology as a purely technical field. In reality, however, technology is an inherently social field, as it involves creating tools and systems that people will use to connect, communicate, and collaborate. Without strong soft skills, even the most technically proficient programmer will struggle to create technology that truly meets users' needs.

Additionally, the fast-paced and often high-pressure nature of the tech industry can create an environment in which soft skills are seen as a luxury rather than a necessity. When there's a constant push to meet deadlines and deliver results, it can be easy to overlook the importance of effective communication, collaboration, and conflict resolution.

But the fact remains that soft skills are essential for success in the tech industry. From effective communication to emotional intelligence to teamwork and leadership, these intangible qualities can make all the difference in a fast-paced, ever-changing field.

For example, consider a team of programmers working on a complex project. If they lack the ability to communicate effectively with one another, they may struggle to coordinate their efforts and end up duplicating work or creating conflicting code. If they lack emotional intelligence, they may struggle to navigate the stresses and pressures of the project, leading to frustration and burnout. And if they lack teamwork and leadership skills, they may struggle to stay focused and motivated as the project progresses.

On the other hand, a team that possesses strong soft skills is far more likely to succeed. They'll be able to communicate clearly and effectively, minimizing confusion and maximizing productivity. They'll be able to support one another emotionally and work collaboratively to overcome obstacles. And they'll be able to stay focused and motivated even when the going gets tough.

Ultimately, the significance of soft skills in the world of technology cannot be overstated. From the simplest app to the most complex system, technology is fundamentally about people - about connecting, communicating, and collaborating in new and innovative ways. And in order to do that successfully, tech professionals need to possess the soft skills that make it all possible.

Chapter One

Understanding Soft Skills

An exploration of the concept of soft skills, including their definition and significance.

In today's world, technology plays an increasingly significant role in virtually every aspect of our lives. From the devices we use to stay connected to the software that powers our workplaces, it's hard to overstate the importance of technology in the 21st century.

And yet, despite this ever-growing reliance on technology, there's a critical component of success in the tech industry that's all too often overlooked: soft skills. These intangible qualities that help individuals connect with others, work collaboratively, and navigate complex social dynamics are often seen as less important than the "hard skills" of programming, data analysis, and technical expertise.

But the truth is that soft skills are every bit as important in the tech industry as they are in any other field. In fact, one could argue that they are even more essential in a world where technology is constantly evolving and the pace of change is faster than ever before.

So why are soft skills so often overlooked in the tech industry? There are a number of reasons, ranging from cultural factors to simple ignorance.

One major factor is the stereotype of the "tech genius" - the idea that the most successful tech professionals are those who possess a natural talent for coding and other technical skills. This stereotype can create a culture in which soft skills are undervalued and even stigmatized.

Another factor is the tendency to view technology as a purely technical field. In reality, however, technology is an inherently social field, as it involves creating tools and systems that people will use to connect, communicate, and collaborate. Without strong soft skills, even the most technically proficient programmer will struggle to create technology that truly meets users' needs.

Additionally, the fast-paced and often high-pressure nature of the tech industry can create an environment in which soft skills are seen as a luxury rather than a necessity. When there's a constant push to meet deadlines and deliver results, it can be easy to overlook the importance of effective communication, collaboration, and conflict resolution.

But the fact remains that soft skills are essential for success in the tech industry. From effective communication to emotional intelligence to teamwork and leadership, these intangible qualities can make all the difference in a fast-paced, ever-changing field.

For example, consider a team of programmers working on a complex project. If they lack the ability to communicate effectively with one another, they may struggle to coordinate their efforts and end up duplicating work or creating conflicting code. If they lack emotional intelligence, they may struggle to navigate the stresses and pressures of the project, leading to frustration and burnout. And if they lack teamwork and leadership skills, they may struggle to stay focused and motivated as the project progresses.

On the other hand, a team that possesses strong soft skills is far more likely to succeed. They'll be able to communicate clearly and effectively, minimizing confusion and maximizing productivity. They'll be able to support one another emotionally and work collaboratively to overcome obstacles. And they'll be able to stay focused and motivated even when the going gets tough.

Ultimately, the significance of soft skills in the world of technology cannot be overstated. From the simplest app to the most complex system, technology is fundamentally about people - about connecting, communicating, and collaborating in new and innovative ways. And in order to do that successfully, tech professionals need to possess the soft skills that make it all possible.

An explanation of how soft skills differ from hard skills, and why both are essential in the world of technology.

T In today's world of work, the terms "soft skills" and "hard skills" are often thrown around interchangeably. However, it is important to understand that these two types of skills are very different, and both are essential for success in the world of technology.

So what exactly are soft skills, and how do they differ from hard skills?

At their most basic level, hard skills refer to technical skills and job-specific knowledge. For example, a software engineer might have hard skills in programming languages like Java or Python, or in data analysis tools like SQL or Tableau.

In contrast, soft skills refer to a set of interpersonal skills that are separate from technical or job-specific skills. These might include things like communication, emotional intelligence, teamwork, leadership, and conflict resolution.

While hard skills are certainly important in many professions, it is often soft skills that distinguish the most successful professionals. In the world of technology, where innovation and disruption are the norm, the ability to adapt and communicate effectively can be the difference between success and failure.

But why are both hard skills and soft skills essential in the world of technology?

On the one hand, hard skills are essential because they allow professionals to perform the technical tasks required for their jobs. In industries like technology, where job-specific knowledge and technical expertise are essential, hard skills are often the first thing that employers look for when hiring new talent.

However, even the most technically skilled professionals will struggle to succeed without strong soft skills. In industries like technology, where collaboration, communication, and teamwork are essential, soft skills are often just as important as hard skills.

For example, a software engineer might be able to write code in multiple programming languages, but if they struggle to communicate effectively with their team or collaborate with other departments, they may struggle to achieve long-term success.

Similarly, a data analyst might be able to perform complex statistical analysis in Python or R, but if they lack strong leadership or conflict resolution skills, they may struggle to effectively communicate their findings or manage relationships with stakeholders.

So how can professionals ensure that they are developing both their hard and soft skills?

One strategy is to focus on building a strong foundation of hard skills, while also intentionally developing soft skills over time. This might involve taking courses or workshops focused on communication, leadership, or emotional intelligence, or seeking out mentorship or coaching to help develop these skills.

Another strategy is to seek out opportunities to practice both hard and soft skills on a regular basis. For example, working on cross-functional teams or participating in team-building exercises can help professionals develop their teamwork and collaboration skills, while also building their technical expertise.

Finally, it is important to recognize that the development of hard and soft skills is an ongoing process that requires continuous learning and improvement. In industries like technology, where the pace of change is so rapid, professionals must be willing to adapt and develop new skills in order to stay competitive.

In conclusion, both hard skills and soft skills are essential for success in the world of technology. While hard skills are important for performing technical tasks and demonstrating job-specific knowledge, soft skills are critical for building effective teams, communicating effectively, and adapting to rapid change. By focusing on the development of both hard and soft skills, professionals can position themselves for long-term success in the years ahead.

A discussion of the most valuable soft skills for IT professionals, and how they can be developed.

In the world of IT, technical skills are undoubtedly important. However, as we have discussed, it is often soft skills that distinguish the most successful professionals. So what are the most valuable soft skills for IT professionals, and how can they be developed?

Communication is perhaps the most important soft skill for IT professionals. In a field where collaboration is key, the ability to communicate effectively with team members, stakeholders, and customers can be the difference between success and failure. Whether through email, chat, or in-person meetings, IT professionals must be able to articulate complex technical ideas in a clear and concise manner.

To develop their communication skills, IT professionals might seek out opportunities to practice public speaking, attend workshops or classes on effective communication, or work with a mentor or coach who can provide feedback and guidance.

Another valuable soft skill for IT professionals is problem-solving. In an industry where the pace of change is rapid and innovation is prized, the ability to think creatively and solve problems is essential. This might involve everything from troubleshooting technical issues to developing new strategies for streamlining workflows or increasing efficiency.

To develop their problem-solving skills, IT professionals might seek out opportunities to work on challenging projects or puzzles, attend workshops or classes on critical thinking, or work with a mentor or coach who can provide guidance and feedback.

Teamwork is another key soft skill for IT professionals. Whether working on cross-functional teams or collaborating with clients and customers, the ability to work well with others is critical. This might involve everything from contributing to brainstorming sessions to building consensus around complex decisions.

To develop their teamwork skills, IT professionals might seek out opportunities to work on team-building exercises or projects, attend workshops or classes on effective collaboration, or work with a mentor or coach who can provide feedback and guidance.

Emotional intelligence is also increasingly important for IT professionals. In an industry where burnout and stress are common, the ability to manage one's own emotions and understand the emotions of others can be essential. This might involve everything from developing self-awareness and self-regulation to building empathy and social skills.

To develop their emotional intelligence, IT professionals might seek out opportunities to practice mindfulness or meditation, attend workshops or classes on emotional intelligence, or work with a mentor or coach who can provide guidance and feedback.

Finally, leadership skills are increasingly important for IT professionals as they advance in their careers. Whether leading teams or driving innovation, the ability to inspire and motivate others is critical. This might involve everything from developing a clear vision and setting goals to building trust and accountability.

To develop their leadership skills, IT professionals might seek out opportunities to take on leadership roles within their organizations or volunteer in their communities, attend workshops or classes on leadership, or work with a mentor or coach who can provide guidance and feedback.

In conclusion, while technical skills are important in the world of IT, it is often soft skills that distinguish the most successful professionals. By focusing on developing their communication, problem-solving, teamwork, emotional intelligence, and leadership skills, IT professionals can position themselves for long-term success in the years ahead.

Chapter Two

Emotional Intelligence

A detailed examination of emotional intelligence, including its definition and components.

Soft skills are a crucial part of every aspect of our lives, including the workplace. They are the interpersonal skills that allow individuals to communicate, collaborate, and build relationships effectively. They include traits such as emotional intelligence, communication, teamwork, leadership, conflict resolution, and creativity, among others. In the fast-paced and constantly evolving world of technology, it is becoming increasingly essential to have well-developed soft skills to succeed in the industry.

Soft skills are often overlooked in favor of technical skills, also known as hard skills, in the technology industry. Hard skills are the skills that are specific to a particular job or field, and they can be taught and measured through various forms of testing. Examples of hard skills include programming, web design, data analysis, and cybersecurity. While hard skills are undoubtedly important in the tech industry, they are not enough on their own to guarantee success. Soft skills are what allow individuals to effectively use their hard skills in the workplace and to collaborate with others to achieve common goals.

One significant difference between hard and soft skills is that hard skills can be taught and learned through formal education and training programs, while soft skills are typically developed over time through experience and personal growth. This is not to say that soft skills cannot be learned and improved upon; they certainly can. However, soft skills require a different approach to learning and development than hard skills do.

Another essential aspect of soft skills is that they are difficult to quantify and measure. Unlike hard skills, which can be assessed through tests and certifications, soft skills are evaluated based on a person's behavior and actions in the workplace. This can make it challenging for employers to assess candidates' soft skills during the hiring process. However, employers are beginning to recognize the importance of soft skills and are starting to incorporate them into their hiring criteria.

In the technology industry, soft skills are becoming increasingly important as the industry becomes more collaborative and teamwork-oriented. The days of the lone programmer working in isolation are long gone. Today's tech companies require teams of professionals working together to develop complex software, analyze data, and solve problems. Soft skills are what allow these teams to function effectively and achieve their goals. Effective communication, for example, is critical to ensure that everyone is on the same page and working towards the same objectives. Leadership and management skills are also essential to ensure that teams are motivated and working efficiently.

Soft skills are also important in the tech industry because they help individuals to adapt to change and innovate. In a rapidly evolving industry, individuals need to be flexible and able to adjust to new technologies and work processes. They need to be able to think creatively and outside of the box to solve problems and develop new products and services. Soft skills such as curiosity, imagination, and creativity can help individuals to do just that.

In conclusion, soft skills are an essential component of success in the technology industry. While hard skills are undoubtedly important, they are not enough on their own to guarantee success. Soft skills are what allow individuals to communicate, collaborate, and build relationships effectively, and to use their hard skills in the workplace. They are challenging to quantify and measure, but they are becoming increasingly important to employers as the industry becomes more collaborative and teamwork-oriented. Soft skills help individuals to adapt to change, innovate, and succeed in their careers. It is essential for individuals in the tech industry to recognize the importance of soft skills and to prioritize their development in order to succeed in this rapidly evolving industry.

An explanation of the benefits of emotional intelligence in the workplace, particularly in the fast-paced world of IT.

In today's fast-paced world of IT, technical skills are often viewed as the primary factor that contributes to success. While technical skills are certainly important, they are not the only skills that matter. Emotional intelligence, or EQ, is a critical component of success in any workplace, but especially in IT, where high-pressure situations and collaboration with diverse teams are common.

So, what exactly is emotional intelligence? At its core, EQ refers to the ability to recognize, understand, and manage one's own emotions, as well as the emotions of others. EQ can be broken down into four components: self-awareness, self-management, social awareness, and relationship management.

In the world of IT, the benefits of emotional intelligence are numerous. One of the most significant benefits is improved communication. IT professionals who possess high EQ are better able to communicate effectively with colleagues, managers, and clients. They are able to listen actively, understand others' perspectives, and respond appropriately. This leads to improved collaboration, better problem-solving, and higher-quality work overall.

Another benefit of emotional intelligence is improved stress management. The world of IT can be incredibly stressful, with tight deadlines, complex projects, and constantly changing priorities. IT professionals with high EQ are better equipped to manage stress in healthy ways, such as through mindfulness practices, exercise, or time management techniques. This, in turn, leads to higher job satisfaction, better job performance, and improved overall well-being.

In addition to improved communication and stress management, emotional intelligence also contributes to better decision-making. IT professionals with high EQ are better able to make decisions based on both logic and empathy. They are able to consider the needs and feelings of others, as well as the overall impact of their decisions. This leads to more thoughtful and effective decision-making, which in turn leads to better business outcomes.

Perhaps most importantly, emotional intelligence contributes to stronger relationships in the workplace. IT professionals with high EQ are able to build trust with colleagues, managers, and clients. They are able to empathize with others, understand their perspectives, and respond in ways that build positive relationships. This is critical in a field like IT, where collaboration and teamwork are essential for success.

While emotional intelligence is certainly an important skill, it is not something that comes naturally to everyone. The good news is that emotional intelligence can be developed and improved over time. One way to do this is through mindfulness practices, such as meditation or breathing exercises. Mindfulness can help IT professionals to become more self-aware, manage their emotions more effectively, and build stronger relationships with others.

Another way to develop emotional intelligence is through practicing active listening. Active listening involves truly listening to what others are saying, without interrupting or thinking about your own response. This can be difficult in the fast-paced world of IT, where time is often of the essence, but it is a skill that can be learned and practiced.

In addition to mindfulness and active listening, there are many other strategies that IT professionals can use to improve their emotional intelligence. These include seeking out feedback from others, practicing empathy, and reflecting on one's own behavior and emotions.

In conclusion, emotional intelligence is a critical skill for success in the world of IT. IT professionals who possess high EQ are better equipped to communicate effectively, manage stress, make thoughtful decisions, and build strong relationships with colleagues, managers, and clients. While emotional intelligence may not come naturally to everyone, it is a skill that can be developed and improved over time. By focusing on developing their emotional intelligence, IT professionals can set themselves up for success in their careers and in life.

A discussion of strategies for improving emotional intelligence, including self-awareness and empathy.

Emotional intelligence is a vital component of success in the workplace, particularly in the fast-paced world of IT. It enables individuals to understand and manage their own emotions while also being attuned to the emotions of others. Those who possess high levels of emotional intelligence can communicate effectively, work well in teams, and handle difficult situations with ease. Fortunately, emotional intelligence is not something that one is born with, but rather it can be developed over time with the right strategies and tools.

One of the most effective strategies for improving emotional intelligence is to develop self-awareness. Self-awareness is the ability to recognize one's own emotions and how they impact others. By increasing self-awareness, individuals can identify their own strengths and weaknesses, understand how their behavior affects others, and develop strategies to manage their emotions effectively. This can be done through various methods, including journaling, self-reflection, and seeking feedback from others.

Another strategy for improving emotional intelligence is to develop empathy. Empathy is the ability to understand and relate to the emotions of others. This skill is particularly important in the world of IT, where individuals must work collaboratively and effectively communicate with others to achieve success. To develop empathy, individuals should actively listen to others, seek to understand their perspectives, and express empathy by acknowledging their emotions. This can be done through various methods, including active listening, asking open-ended questions, and practicing perspective-taking exercises.

In addition to self-awareness and empathy, there are several other strategies for improving emotional intelligence. These include:

1. Mindfulness: Mindfulness is the practice of being present in the moment and observing one's thoughts and feelings without judgment. By practicing mindfulness, individuals can develop greater self-awareness and the ability to manage their emotions effectively. This can be done through various methods, including meditation, breathing exercises, and yoga.

2. Emotional regulation: Emotional regulation is the ability to manage one's own emotions effectively. This includes the ability to recognize and label emotions, understand the triggers that lead to emotional reactions, and develop strategies for managing these reactions. Techniques for emotional regulation include

deep breathing, progressive muscle relaxation, and cognitive restructuring.

3. Social skills: Social skills are the ability to communicate effectively, build relationships, and work collaboratively with others. Developing social skills involves practicing active listening, expressing empathy, and adapting communication style to suit different situations and personalities. Other techniques for developing social skills include role-playing, group discussions, and team-building exercises.

4. Continuous learning: Emotional intelligence is not something that can be developed overnight, but rather it requires ongoing learning and practice. Individuals can develop emotional intelligence by seeking out opportunities for learning, practicing new skills, and seeking feedback from others. This can be done through various methods, including attending training sessions, reading books, and seeking feedback from mentors or colleagues.

In conclusion, emotional intelligence is a vital skill for success in the workplace, particularly in the fast-paced world of IT. Fortunately, emotional intelligence is not something that one is born with, but rather it can be developed over time with the right strategies and tools. By developing self-awareness, empathy, mindfulness, emotional regulation, social skills, and a commitment to continuous learning, individuals can improve their emotional intelligence and achieve greater success in their careers.

Chapter Three

Communication

An exploration of the importance of effective communication in the workplace, with particular emphasis on the tech industry.

Effective communication is essential in every workplace, but it is particularly important in the fast-paced world of technology. In the tech industry, communication breakdowns can result in delays, misunderstandings, and even project failures. This is because technology professionals often work on complex projects that require collaboration between multiple team members, departments, and even external stakeholders. Without effective communication, team members may not be able to convey their ideas, goals, and expectations to each other, which can lead to confusion and frustration.

Effective communication is not just about transmitting information; it is also about ensuring that the message is received and understood by the recipient. This requires careful attention to the medium of communication, the tone of the message, and the intended audience. In the tech industry, communication can take many forms, including email, instant messaging, video conferencing, and face-to-face meetings. Each of these communication channels has its strengths and weaknesses, and it is important to choose the most appropriate channel for the message you want to convey.

One of the most significant challenges in the tech industry is the use of technical jargon and acronyms, which can be confusing for those who are not familiar with the terminology. This is where the importance of effective communication becomes even more critical. It is essential to use clear and concise language when communicating technical information, and to take the time to explain any unfamiliar terms or concepts to those who may not be familiar with them.

Another important aspect of effective communication in the tech industry is the ability to convey complex technical ideas to non-technical stakeholders. This requires the use of plain language and visual aids, such as diagrams and infographics. By presenting technical information in a way that is easily understandable to non-technical stakeholders, technology professionals can build trust and credibility with their clients and customers.

Finally, effective communication in the tech industry also requires active listening skills. This means being present and fully engaged in the conversation, asking questions to clarify any misunderstandings, and demonstrating empathy for the other person's point of view. By actively listening to others, technology professionals can build stronger relationships and foster a culture of collaboration and respect.

In conclusion, effective communication is essential in the tech industry, as it allows team members to collaborate effectively, avoid misunderstandings, and achieve project goals. Technology professionals must take the time to choose the most appropriate communication channel for their message, use clear and concise language, and actively listen to others. By doing so, they can build trust, credibility, and strong working relationships, which are essential for success in the fast-paced world of technology.

A discussion of verbal and nonverbal communication skills, and how they can be improved.

Effective communication is crucial for success in any industry, but it is especially important in the fast-paced world of technology. Communication breakdowns can lead to project delays, misunderstandings, and even lost business opportunities. That's why it's essential for IT professionals to not only understand the importance of communication but also develop their verbal and nonverbal communication skills.

Verbal communication skills are the most obvious aspect of communication, and they refer to the use of language to convey information. In the tech industry, where complex technical concepts are the norm, clear and concise language is crucial. However, technical jargon can often be a barrier to effective communication, especially when communicating with non-technical stakeholders. Therefore, IT professionals should be able to simplify complex technical terms and concepts for the layman.

Another important aspect of verbal communication is active listening. Active listening involves fully concentrating on what the speaker is saying and providing feedback to show that you have understood. It's not uncommon in the tech industry for people to interrupt or cut each other off mid-sentence, especially when discussing technical topics. Active listening involves resisting the urge to interrupt and instead focusing on what the speaker is saying.

In addition to verbal communication skills, nonverbal communication is equally important. Nonverbal communication includes body language, tone of voice, and facial expressions. It's been said that up to 90% of communication is nonverbal, which makes it an essential aspect of communication in the tech industry.

One of the most critical nonverbal communication skills is maintaining eye contact. When you look someone in the eye, it shows that you are paying attention and are fully engaged in the conversation. On the other hand, avoiding eye contact can come across as uninterested or disengaged.

Facial expressions are another essential aspect of nonverbal communication. Our facial expressions can convey a lot of information, and they can be used to show emotions such as happiness, sadness, anger, or surprise. In the tech industry, where the focus is often on technical tasks and deadlines, it's easy to forget the importance of showing emotions. However, conveying emotions can help build better relationships with colleagues and clients.

Finally, body language is another critical aspect of nonverbal communication. Our body language can convey confidence, openness, and interest. For example, standing up straight and maintaining an open posture can convey confidence and openness. In contrast, crossing your arms or slouching can convey a lack of interest or defensiveness.

Fortunately, improving both verbal and nonverbal communication skills is achievable with the right strategies. One of the most effective ways to improve communication skills is to practice active listening. This involves paying full attention to what the speaker is saying, paraphrasing their words to ensure understanding, and asking clarifying questions.

Another strategy for improving communication skills is to seek feedback from colleagues and clients. This can help you identify areas for improvement and gain a better understanding of how others perceive your communication style.

In addition, taking courses or attending workshops on communication can help improve communication skills. These courses can cover topics such as public speaking, active listening, and conflict resolution, which can all contribute to better communication in the workplace.

Finally, practicing good body language is another effective way to improve communication skills. This can involve standing up straight, maintaining eye contact, and using open body language to convey confidence and openness.

In conclusion, effective communication is an essential skill for success in the tech industry. Verbal and nonverbal communication skills are both crucial aspects of communication, and both can be improved with practice and effort. By developing these skills, IT professionals can improve their relationships with colleagues and clients, avoid misunderstandings, and ultimately succeed in their careers.

Techniques for navigating communication challenges and building better working relationships.

Effective communication is essential for building strong relationships and achieving success in any workplace, and the tech industry is no exception. However, despite its importance, communication can be challenging, especially in the fast-paced, high-pressure world of technology. Fortunately, there are techniques that can help navigate these challenges and build better working relationships.

One important technique is active listening. Active listening involves paying close attention to the speaker, asking clarifying questions, and summarizing what has been said to ensure mutual understanding. It is a critical skill for building rapport, understanding the needs and concerns of others, and resolving conflicts. When actively listening, it's important to focus on the speaker and avoid distractions, such as checking emails or scrolling through social media.

Another technique for navigating communication challenges is being aware of cultural differences. In the tech industry, teams are often composed of individuals from diverse backgrounds, cultures, and languages. Being aware of these differences and making an effort to understand and respect them can help avoid misunderstandings and build stronger relationships. This can involve learning about different communication styles, nonverbal cues, and language barriers.

It's also important to be mindful of one's own communication style and how it may be perceived by others. This includes both verbal and nonverbal cues, such as tone of voice, body language, and facial expressions. For example, using a harsh tone of voice can make others feel defensive, while a smile or nod can convey warmth and understanding. Additionally, being aware of the impact of technology on communication, such as the potential for misinterpretation in written messages, can help avoid misunderstandings and build better relationships.

Conflict resolution is another area where effective communication is critical. When conflicts arise, it's important to address them openly and honestly, rather than avoiding them or letting them escalate. One technique for conflict resolution is active listening, as mentioned previously. Another technique is seeking to understand the other person's perspective and finding common ground. This can involve asking open-ended questions, avoiding blame, and focusing on solutions rather than problems. Additionally, using "I" statements rather than "you" statements can help keep the conversation focused on feelings and needs, rather than assigning blame.

Another technique for building better working relationships is giving and receiving feedback. Feedback is essential for personal and professional growth, but it can be challenging to deliver and receive effectively. When giving feedback, it's important to be specific, objective, and constructive, while avoiding personal attacks or judgment. When receiving feedback, it's important to listen actively and be open to criticism, rather than becoming defensive or dismissive.

Finally, building better working relationships involves building trust. Trust is critical for effective communication, collaboration, and problem-solving. One technique for building trust is being reliable and following through on commitments. This involves being honest about what can be accomplished, setting realistic expectations, and communicating clearly about progress and challenges. Additionally, being transparent and authentic can help build trust by showing vulnerability and creating a sense of shared experience.

In conclusion, effective communication is essential for building strong relationships and achieving success in the tech industry. Techniques such as active listening, cultural awareness, and feedback can help navigate communication challenges and build better working relationships. By being mindful of one's own communication style, seeking to understand others, and building trust, individuals in the tech industry can cultivate a culture of effective communication, collaboration, and innovation.

Chapter Four

Collaboration and Teamwork

The significance of collaboration and teamwork in IT, and the challenges that can arise.

Collaboration and teamwork are essential elements for success in the fast-paced world of IT. With complex projects and ever-changing technologies, it's important for IT professionals to work together in a cohesive and efficient manner. The significance of collaboration and teamwork in IT cannot be overstated, as it can lead to increased productivity, innovation, and overall success.

However, collaboration and teamwork can be challenging. With differing personalities, work styles, and skillsets, conflicts and misunderstandings can arise. In addition, IT professionals often work remotely or across different time zones, making it difficult to establish effective communication and work together seamlessly.

One of the biggest challenges in collaboration and teamwork is communication. Effective communication is key to ensuring that everyone is on the same page and working towards the same goals. This includes clear communication of deadlines, expectations, and feedback. Miscommunication can lead to missed deadlines, confusion, and even project failure.

Another challenge is the lack of accountability. When working in a team, it can be easy to assume that someone else will take care of a particular task or responsibility. This can lead to missed deadlines, incomplete work, and frustration among team members. It's important for each team member to take ownership of their role and responsibilities, and for the team as a whole to establish a system of accountability.

Another challenge in collaboration and teamwork is the potential for conflicts to arise. With different personalities and perspectives, conflicts can arise over differing opinions, priorities, and approaches to work. This can lead to tension and a breakdown in communication, which can ultimately impact the success of the project.

Despite these challenges, the benefits of collaboration and teamwork in IT are numerous. Collaboration allows for the pooling of resources and knowledge, leading to increased productivity and efficiency. It also fosters innovation and creativity, as team members can bounce ideas off each other and build upon one another's strengths. Collaboration can also lead to greater job satisfaction, as team members feel supported and valued by their colleagues.

Teamwork is also crucial in IT, as it allows for the division of labor and the delegation of tasks. By dividing responsibilities among team members, projects can be completed more quickly and efficiently. Teamwork also allows for the sharing of expertise and knowledge, as team members can learn from each other and build upon each other's strengths.

To overcome the challenges of collaboration and teamwork in IT, it's important to establish clear goals and expectations from the outset. This includes clear communication of deadlines, roles and responsibilities, and project objectives. It's also important to establish a system of accountability, so that each team member understands their role and responsibilities, and is held responsible for completing them.

Effective communication is also key to successful collaboration and teamwork. This includes regular check-ins and updates, clear communication of expectations and feedback, and a willingness to listen to and address concerns and issues as they arise. It's also important to establish a system for conflict resolution, so that conflicts can be addressed and resolved in a timely and effective manner.

In conclusion, the significance of collaboration and teamwork in IT cannot be overstated. While there are challenges to effective collaboration and teamwork, the benefits are numerous. Collaboration and teamwork allow for increased productivity, innovation, and job satisfaction, and are essential for success in the fast-paced world of IT. By establishing clear goals and expectations, effective communication, and a system of accountability and conflict resolution, IT professionals can overcome the challenges of collaboration and teamwork and achieve success in their projects.

Techniques for effective collaboration and teamwork, including project management tools and effective communication.

Effective collaboration and teamwork are critical components of success in the world of IT. But simply recognizing their importance is not enough – it is essential to have the right tools and strategies in place to ensure that collaboration and teamwork can thrive.

One essential technique for effective collaboration and teamwork is the use of project management tools. In today's tech industry, there are a plethora of project management tools available that can help teams stay organized, communicate effectively, and stay on track with project timelines. Some popular tools include Asana, Trello, Jira, and Basecamp, to name just a few.

These tools enable teams to break down complex projects into smaller, more manageable tasks, assign responsibilities to specific team members, set deadlines, and track progress. By using project management tools, teams can ensure that everyone is on the same page, and that everyone knows what is expected of them at each stage of the project.

Another key technique for effective collaboration and teamwork is effective communication. Clear and open communication is critical for any team to work together effectively, but it is particularly important in the tech industry, where teams often work remotely or across different time zones.

To promote effective communication, teams should establish clear communication channels and protocols. This can include using tools like Slack or Microsoft Teams for instant messaging, setting up regular team meetings, and establishing guidelines for how and when team members should communicate with one another.

In addition to these tools, there are several best practices that teams can follow to promote effective communication. First and foremost, team members should be encouraged to ask questions and seek clarification whenever they are unsure about something. This can help prevent misunderstandings and ensure that everyone is on the same page.

Secondly, it is important to establish a culture of openness and transparency. This means encouraging team members to share their thoughts and ideas openly, and to be willing to listen to and incorporate feedback from others.

Finally, it is critical to ensure that communication is respectful and professional at all times. This means avoiding confrontational or aggressive language, and instead focusing on finding solutions and working together as a team.

In addition to project management tools and effective communication, there are several other techniques that teams can use to promote collaboration and teamwork. One key strategy is to establish a sense of shared ownership and accountability for projects. This means encouraging team members to take ownership of their work, and to be accountable for the results.

Another technique is to establish a culture of collaboration, where team members are encouraged to work together to solve problems and find solutions. This can involve setting up cross-functional teams that bring together individuals from different departments or areas of expertise, or establishing regular brainstorming sessions where team members can share ideas and insights.

Ultimately, the key to effective collaboration and teamwork is to establish a culture of trust and respect, where team members feel comfortable working together and sharing their thoughts and ideas. This requires strong leadership and a commitment to ongoing improvement, as well as a willingness to invest in the tools and techniques that are necessary for success.

In conclusion, effective collaboration and teamwork are essential components of success in the world of IT. By using project management tools, promoting effective communication, and establishing a culture of shared ownership and collaboration, teams can work together more effectively and achieve better results. As the tech industry continues to evolve and change, it is critical that IT professionals continue to prioritize collaboration and teamwork, and that they stay up-to-date with the latest tools and techniques for promoting these essential skills.

Strategies for improving collaboration and teamwork skills in the workplace.

Collaboration and teamwork are essential skills for success in any workplace, but particularly in the fast-paced world of technology. The ability to work effectively with others, communicate ideas, and delegate tasks can lead to more efficient workflows and ultimately better outcomes. However, it can be challenging to develop these skills, especially in a workplace where everyone has different work styles and personalities. Here are some strategies for improving collaboration and teamwork skills in the workplace.

1. Establish clear goals and roles One of the most important things you can do to improve collaboration and teamwork is to ensure that everyone understands the goals of the project and their individual roles in achieving them. This can help to avoid confusion and

misunderstandings, and also ensures that everyone is working towards a common purpose.

2. Encourage open communication Effective communication is key to successful collaboration and teamwork. Encourage team members to express their ideas, concerns, and feedback openly and honestly. Provide opportunities for team members to share their thoughts and feelings, whether through regular team meetings or one-on-one conversations.

3. Use project management tools There are many project management tools available that can help to streamline workflows and facilitate collaboration. Tools like Trello, Asana, and Basecamp can help to assign tasks, set deadlines, and track progress. By using these tools, team members can easily see what others are working on and stay informed about project updates.

4. Foster a culture of trust and respect Collaboration and teamwork require trust and respect between team members. Encourage team members to treat each other with respect and empathy, and to be supportive of each other's ideas and contributions. When team members feel valued and supported, they are more likely to work well together and produce better outcomes.

5. Set clear expectations for communication and feedback To improve collaboration and teamwork, it is important to set clear expectations for communication and feedback. Let team members know when and how they should communicate with each other, and establish guidelines for providing feedback. This can help to

ensure that communication is effective and productive, rather than confusing or counterproductive.

6. Encourage collaboration outside of work Encouraging team members to socialize and collaborate outside of work can help to build stronger working relationships. Consider organizing team-building activities or social events, or encouraging team members to meet outside of work to work on projects or discuss ideas.

7. Provide opportunities for training and development Finally, providing opportunities for training and development can help team members to improve their collaboration and teamwork skills. Consider offering training sessions or workshops on topics like communication, leadership, and conflict resolution. By investing in the development of your team members, you can help to build a stronger, more effective team.

In conclusion, collaboration and teamwork are critical skills for success in the fast-paced world of technology. By establishing clear goals and roles, encouraging open communication, using project management tools, fostering a culture of trust and respect, setting clear expectations for communication and feedback, encouraging collaboration outside of work, and providing opportunities for training and development, you can improve collaboration and teamwork skills in the workplace. With these strategies in place, your team can work more effectively together, produce better outcomes, and ultimately achieve greater success.

Chapter Five

Leadership and Management

An examination of the role of leadership and management in the tech industry.

Leadership and management play crucial roles in the success of any organization, and the tech industry is no exception. The rapidly changing nature of technology and the dynamic environment of the tech industry demand strong leadership and management skills. In this chapter, we will examine the role of leadership and management in the tech industry and explore how these skills can be honed for success.

Effective leadership in the tech industry involves the ability to provide direction and guidance to a team while navigating the ever-changing technological landscape. Leaders must be able to identify and prioritize goals, establish a vision, and develop strategies to achieve success. They must also be able to inspire and motivate their team to work towards common goals.

Effective management in the tech industry involves overseeing the day-to-day operations of a team, ensuring that projects are completed on time and within budget, and managing resources effectively. Managers must be able to delegate tasks, provide feedback and support to team members, and make decisions that balance the needs of the organization with those of the team.

One of the biggest challenges faced by leaders and managers in the tech industry is the fast-paced and constantly evolving nature of technology. This requires leaders and managers to be adaptable, flexible, and able to pivot quickly in response to changes in the industry.

Another challenge is managing a team of highly skilled and technical individuals who often have specialized knowledge in different areas. Leaders and managers must be able to effectively communicate with their team, understand their individual strengths and weaknesses, and delegate tasks accordingly. They must also be able to foster an environment of collaboration and teamwork, where team members can work together to achieve common goals.

There are several key skills that are essential for effective leadership and management in the tech industry. These include:

1. Communication: Effective communication is essential for leaders and managers to convey their vision and goals to their team, provide feedback and support, and ensure that everyone is working towards common objectives. This includes both verbal and written communication skills.

2. Adaptability: Leaders and managers in the tech industry must be able to adapt quickly to changes in the industry and the needs of the organization. This requires a willingness to learn and a flexible approach to problem-solving.

3. Emotional Intelligence: Emotional intelligence involves the ability to understand and manage one's own

emotions, as well as the emotions of others. This is particularly important in the tech industry, where high-stress environments and tight deadlines can lead to tensions and conflicts within teams.

4. Decision-making: Leaders and managers must be able to make decisions that balance the needs of the organization with those of the team, and that are based on data and sound reasoning.

5. Delegation: Effective delegation involves identifying the strengths and weaknesses of team members and assigning tasks accordingly. This helps to ensure that projects are completed efficiently and that team members are engaged and challenged in their work.

To improve their leadership and management skills, tech professionals can participate in training programs and seek out mentorship opportunities. They can also network with other professionals in the industry and seek feedback from their team members and colleagues.

In conclusion, effective leadership and management are essential for success in the tech industry. Leaders and managers must be able to navigate the rapidly changing technological landscape, foster collaboration and teamwork, and manage highly skilled and technical individuals. Developing key skills such as communication, adaptability, emotional intelligence, decision-making, and delegation can help tech professionals to excel in leadership and management roles.

An overview of different leadership and management styles and their impact on team performance.

Leadership and management styles have a significant impact on the performance of a team in any industry, including the tech industry. A leader's style can affect employee motivation, productivity, and job satisfaction, which ultimately affect the success of the organization.

There are several leadership and management styles, each with its strengths and weaknesses. A leader can use one or a combination of styles, depending on the situation and the team's needs. Here is an overview of some of the most common leadership and management styles and their impact on team performance:

1. Autocratic leadership: Autocratic leadership is characterized by a centralized decision-making process in which the leader makes all the decisions and directs the team's work. This leadership style can be effective in emergencies or situations where quick decisions need to be made. However, it can lead to employee disengagement, low morale, and high turnover rates.

2. Democratic leadership: Democratic leadership is characterized by a participatory decision-making process, in which the leader involves the team members in the decision-making process. This style can lead to higher job satisfaction and better employee engagement, as employees feel valued and involved in the decision-making process. However, it can be time-

consuming and ineffective in situations where quick decisions need to be made.

3. Laissez-faire leadership: Laissez-faire leadership is characterized by a hands-off approach, in which the leader delegates tasks and responsibilities to team members, and the team members have a high degree of autonomy. This leadership style can be effective in situations where the team members are experienced and self-motivated. However, it can lead to a lack of direction and accountability, which can negatively impact team performance.

4. Transformational leadership: Transformational leadership is characterized by a leader who inspires and motivates the team members to achieve their best work. This leadership style can lead to increased employee engagement, job satisfaction, and productivity. However, it can be time-consuming and requires a high degree of emotional intelligence and interpersonal skills.

5. Transactional leadership: Transactional leadership is characterized by a leader who uses rewards and punishments to motivate team members. This leadership style can be effective in situations where the team members are motivated by rewards or fear of punishment. However, it can lead to low employee engagement and job satisfaction, as team members may feel like they are being treated like cogs in a machine.

6. Servant leadership: Servant leadership is characterized by a leader who prioritizes the needs of the team members over their own needs. This leadership style

can lead to increased trust, loyalty, and job satisfaction among team members. However, it can be challenging to implement, as it requires a high degree of selflessness and humility.

The choice of leadership and management style should depend on the organization's culture, goals, and the team's needs. It is essential to assess the team's dynamics and identify the leadership style that would be most effective in achieving the organization's goals.

In conclusion, leadership and management styles have a significant impact on team performance in the tech industry. There are several leadership and management styles, each with its strengths and weaknesses. A leader should choose a leadership style that is appropriate for the situation and the team's needs. Effective leadership can lead to increased employee engagement, job satisfaction, and productivity, while ineffective leadership can lead to low morale, employee disengagement, and high turnover rates.

Techniques for improving leadership and management skills, including delegation, mentorship, and feedback.

Effective leadership and management are essential for the success of any organization, especially in the fast-paced world of technology. Leaders and managers in the tech industry must possess a variety of skills, including the ability to delegate tasks, provide mentorship to team members, and give and receive feedback. Here are some techniques for improving leadership and management skills in the workplace:

1. Delegation: Delegation is a crucial skill for leaders and managers in the tech industry. Effective delegation involves identifying the right person for the job, providing clear instructions, and establishing a timeline for completion. It also involves providing support and guidance to the person undertaking the task. Delegation can help managers focus on higher-level tasks while empowering their team members to develop new skills and take on new challenges.

2. Mentorship: Providing mentorship to team members is a great way for leaders and managers to help their employees develop their skills and reach their full potential. Mentorship involves establishing a relationship of trust and support with a team member and providing guidance, feedback, and support as they work to achieve their goals. Effective mentorship can lead to increased job satisfaction, improved job performance, and reduced employee turnover.

3. Feedback: Giving and receiving feedback is an essential aspect of effective leadership and management in the tech industry. Leaders and managers must be able to provide constructive feedback to their team members, highlighting areas for improvement and providing guidance on how to improve performance. Similarly, they must be open to receiving feedback from their team members, taking it into consideration, and using it to improve their leadership and management skills.

4. Continuous learning: Leadership and management skills are not static; they must be continually developed and refined. Leaders and managers in the tech industry

must be committed to continuous learning, staying up to date on the latest trends and best practices in their field, and seeking out opportunities for professional development. This can include attending conferences, taking courses or workshops, and reading industry publications.

5. Empathy: Empathy is a critical leadership and management skill that can help leaders build trust and establish strong working relationships with their team members. Empathy involves the ability to understand and share the feelings of others, putting oneself in their shoes and seeing things from their perspective. Leaders who demonstrate empathy are better able to communicate with their team members, build trust, and motivate them to perform at their best.

6. Time management: Effective time management is another crucial leadership and management skill. Leaders and managers in the tech industry must be able to prioritize tasks, manage their time effectively, and ensure that their team members are also managing their time effectively. This involves setting clear goals and deadlines, establishing processes and procedures for completing tasks, and tracking progress and outcomes.

In conclusion, effective leadership and management are essential for the success of any organization, particularly in the tech industry. Leaders and managers must possess a variety of skills, including the ability to delegate tasks, provide mentorship to team members, give and receive feedback, continuously learn, demonstrate empathy, and manage their time effectively. By honing these skills and continually striving to improve, leaders and managers can create a positive work environment, build strong relationships with their team members, and drive success for their organization.

Chapter Six

Conflict Resolution

An exploration of the conflicts that can arise in the tech industry and how they can be resolved.

Conflicts are inevitable in any workplace, and the tech industry is no exception. However, due to the fast-paced, high-pressure environment of the tech industry, conflicts can be particularly challenging to resolve. It's essential for IT professionals to be equipped with conflict resolution skills to handle conflicts constructively and maintain positive working relationships with colleagues. In this section, we will explore the types of conflicts that can arise in the tech industry and some techniques for resolving them.

One of the most common sources of conflict in the tech industry is disagreements over project timelines or priorities. For example, if two team members have different ideas about how a project should be completed or disagree on the order of tasks, this can lead to conflict. In such cases, it's essential to focus on the common goal and work collaboratively to find a mutually agreeable solution. This may involve brainstorming ideas, evaluating each suggestion's pros and cons, and finding a compromise that satisfies both parties.

Another source of conflict in the tech industry is differences in working styles or communication styles. For example, if one team member prefers to work independently and another prefers to work collaboratively, this can lead to misunderstandings and tension. In such cases, it's important to recognize and respect each person's working style and find ways to bridge the gap. This may involve setting clear expectations and boundaries for communication and collaboration or finding alternative ways to work together that accommodate different styles.

Personality clashes can also lead to conflict in the tech industry. For example, if two team members have very different personalities, they may find it challenging to work together. In such cases, it's important to be aware of each person's strengths and weaknesses and find ways to complement each other's skills. This may involve delegating tasks based on each person's strengths or finding ways to balance each other's personalities to create a more harmonious working relationship.

Regardless of the source of the conflict, it's crucial to approach conflict resolution with a positive and constructive attitude. This involves active listening, empathy, and a willingness to compromise. It's important to avoid becoming defensive or confrontational, as this can escalate the conflict further. Instead, try to approach the situation with an open mind and a willingness to work together to find a mutually agreeable solution.

Mediation is one technique that can be effective in resolving conflicts in the tech industry. This involves a neutral third party who works with both parties to facilitate communication and find a mutually agreeable solution. Mediation can be particularly helpful in cases where there is a significant power imbalance or where the conflict is particularly complex or emotionally charged.

Negotiation is another technique that can be effective in resolving conflicts in the tech industry. This involves a process of give and take, where both parties work together to find a compromise that satisfies both their interests. Negotiation can be particularly helpful in cases where there are limited resources or conflicting priorities.

Finally, it's important to remember that conflict resolution is an ongoing process. It's not a one-time event but rather an ongoing effort to maintain positive working relationships and address conflicts constructively as they arise. This involves ongoing communication, feedback, and a willingness to adapt and grow together as a team.

In conclusion, conflicts are inevitable in the tech industry, but they can be effectively resolved with the right skills and techniques. By focusing on common goals, respecting each other's working styles and personalities, and approaching conflict resolution with a positive and constructive attitude, IT professionals can maintain positive working relationships and achieve success as a team. It's essential to approach conflict resolution as an ongoing process and be willing to adapt and grow together as a team.

Techniques for effective conflict resolution, including mediation and negotiation.

In any workplace, conflicts are inevitable, and the tech industry is no exception. Conflicts can arise from a variety of sources, including differences in personality, communication styles, or working methods. Therefore, it is crucial for employees to learn techniques for effective conflict resolution. In this article, we will explore some techniques for resolving conflicts in the workplace, including mediation and negotiation.

Mediation is a process of resolving conflicts with the help of a neutral third party. The mediator's role is to facilitate communication between the conflicting parties, identify areas of agreement and disagreement, and help the parties reach a mutually acceptable solution. Mediation can be a highly effective way to resolve conflicts because it allows the parties to reach a resolution without resorting to formal grievance procedures, which can be time-consuming, expensive, and emotionally draining.

One of the key advantages of mediation is that it is voluntary. The parties can choose whether or not to participate in the process, and they are free to leave at any time. This is important because it helps to ensure that the parties are invested in finding a resolution and are committed to working together to resolve the conflict.

Another advantage of mediation is that it is confidential. The mediator will not share any information about the process or the parties involved with anyone outside of the mediation. This can be especially important in the tech industry, where confidentiality is often critical to the success of the business.

Negotiation is another technique for resolving conflicts in the workplace. Negotiation is a process in which the parties involved in the conflict work together to find a mutually acceptable solution. Unlike mediation, negotiation is not facilitated by a neutral third party. Instead, the parties themselves are responsible for finding a resolution.

One of the key advantages of negotiation is that it can be a more efficient way to resolve conflicts than formal grievance procedures. Negotiation allows the parties to work together to find a solution that meets everyone's needs, rather than relying on a third party to make a decision for them.

Effective negotiation requires good communication skills. The parties involved in the conflict must be able to express their needs and interests clearly and listen to each other's perspectives. They must also be able to identify areas of agreement and disagreement and work together to find a resolution that meets everyone's needs.

One of the key challenges of negotiation is that it can be difficult to find a resolution that satisfies everyone. Sometimes, the parties involved in the conflict have fundamentally different needs or interests that cannot be reconciled. In these cases, it may be necessary to involve a neutral third party, such as a mediator, to help the parties find a resolution.

In conclusion, conflict resolution is an essential skill for employees in the tech industry. Mediation and negotiation are two techniques that can be highly effective for resolving conflicts in the workplace. Mediation allows the parties to reach a resolution with the help of a neutral third party, while negotiation allows the parties to work together to find a mutually acceptable solution. Effective conflict resolution requires good communication skills and a willingness to work together to find a resolution that meets everyone's needs. By developing these skills, employees in the tech industry can help to create a more harmonious and productive workplace.

Strategies for improving conflict resolution skills in the workplace.

In today's fast-paced world, it can be challenging to balance work and personal life. However, achieving work-life balance is crucial to maintaining one's physical and mental health, relationships, and overall happiness. In the tech industry, where work often demands long hours and continuous learning, achieving work-life balance can be even more challenging. It requires dedication, planning, and a proactive approach.

One of the most important strategies for achieving work-life balance is effective time management. Time is a precious commodity, and it's essential to make the most of it. One way to do this is to create a schedule or a to-do list that prioritizes tasks based on their importance and urgency. It's important to allocate time for work, personal obligations, and leisure activities, such as hobbies or exercise.

Another technique for achieving work-life balance is to set boundaries between work and personal life. This means establishing clear working hours and avoiding working outside of those hours, except in exceptional circumstances. It also means disconnecting from work-related technology, such as email or instant messaging, during non-working hours. This allows for time to recharge and focus on personal life.

Self-care is also essential in achieving work-life balance. It's crucial to take care of oneself physically, emotionally, and mentally. This can involve activities such as exercise, healthy eating, mindfulness practices, and engaging in hobbies or activities that bring joy and relaxation. Additionally, it's important to prioritize sleep and take breaks throughout the day to recharge and refocus.

Finally, seeking support from friends, family, or colleagues can be beneficial in achieving work-life balance. It's essential to communicate with others about one's needs and to seek help when necessary. This can involve delegating tasks at work, seeking guidance or mentorship, or seeking help with personal responsibilities.

In conclusion, achieving work-life balance is critical for maintaining physical and mental health, relationships, and overall happiness. Effective time management, setting boundaries, prioritizing self-care, and seeking support are all key strategies for achieving work-life balance in the fast-paced world of IT. By proactively taking steps to achieve work-life balance, individuals can improve their well-being and overall quality of life.

Chapter Seven

Work-Life Balance and Well-Being

An examination of the importance of work-life balance and well-being in the fast-paced world of IT.

The world of technology moves at a rapid pace, and the demands placed on IT professionals are often intense. Long hours, tight deadlines, and a constant need for innovation can make it difficult for those in the industry to achieve a healthy work-life balance. However, prioritizing work-life balance and well-being is essential for both personal health and professional success.

Research has shown that overworking can lead to burnout, a state of emotional, mental, and physical exhaustion that can impact one's ability to perform effectively on the job. This is particularly relevant in the tech industry, where the pressure to constantly innovate and keep up with the latest trends can be overwhelming. Without adequate rest and time for self-care, IT professionals may find themselves struggling to keep up with the demands of their job.

Achieving work-life balance is crucial for maintaining mental and physical health, but it can also improve job performance. When employees feel rested and refreshed, they are more productive, creative, and engaged in their work. On the other hand, when employees are constantly stressed and overworked, they are more likely to make mistakes, experience decreased job satisfaction, and ultimately, burn out.

One way to achieve work-life balance is to prioritize time management. Many IT professionals work in a deadline-driven environment, but it's essential to set aside time for self-care and relaxation. This can include taking breaks throughout the day, scheduling time for exercise, and unplugging from work outside of business hours. By prioritizing time management, IT professionals can avoid the trap of constant overworking and create a more balanced lifestyle.

Another crucial component of achieving work-life balance is practicing self-care. This can take many forms, from physical activities such as exercise and healthy eating to mental wellness practices such as meditation and therapy. Self-care allows individuals to recharge and reduce stress levels, which can have a positive impact on both personal and professional life.

In addition to prioritizing work-life balance and self-care, it's also important for IT companies to promote well-being in the workplace. This can include offering wellness programs, creating a culture of open communication and support, and encouraging employees to take breaks and prioritize their mental and physical health. By fostering a workplace that values well-being, companies can help prevent burnout and create a happier, more productive workforce.

In conclusion, work-life balance and well-being are crucial components of success in the fast-paced world of IT. Prioritizing time management, practicing self-care, and fostering a culture of well-being in the workplace can lead to increased job satisfaction, improved performance, and ultimately, a more successful career. By taking care of ourselves, we can better take care of our work and achieve the balance necessary for personal and professional growth.

Strategies for achieving work-life balance, including time management and self-care.

In today's fast-paced world, achieving work-life balance can be a significant challenge. This is especially true for those working in the tech industry, where long hours and high-pressure deadlines are the norm. However, maintaining a healthy work-life balance is essential for preventing burnout, maintaining mental and physical health, and achieving long-term success. In this chapter, we will explore some strategies for achieving work-life balance, including time management and self-care.

Time management is a critical aspect of achieving work-life balance. Effective time management means being able to prioritize tasks, manage your schedule, and make time for both work and personal life. One effective technique for managing your time is to create a schedule or to-do list for each day. This can help you stay organized and ensure that you are making progress towards your goals. It is also important to set realistic goals and deadlines for yourself, as this can help you avoid overworking and feeling overwhelmed.

Another useful strategy for achieving work-life balance is self-care. Self-care means taking care of your physical, emotional, and mental health. This can include things like exercise, meditation, spending time with loved ones, and engaging in hobbies and interests outside of work. Self-care is essential for preventing burnout and maintaining good mental health. When you take care of yourself, you are better equipped to handle the challenges of work and daily life.

One important aspect of self-care is taking breaks throughout the day. It can be tempting to work straight through the day without taking breaks, especially when deadlines are looming. However, taking regular breaks can actually make you more productive and help you avoid burnout. Consider taking a short walk or doing some stretching exercises during your breaks. This can help you clear your mind and recharge your batteries.

In addition to taking breaks, it is also important to set boundaries between work and personal life. This can be challenging, especially if you are used to checking work emails or taking calls outside of work hours. However, setting boundaries can help you create a clear separation between work and personal time, allowing you to focus on your personal life and recharge your batteries. Consider turning off work-related notifications during non-work hours or designating certain times of the day as "unplugged" time.

Finally, it is important to ask for help when you need it. This can mean delegating tasks at work or seeking support from friends and family outside of work. It is okay to admit when you are feeling overwhelmed or when you need assistance. Seeking help can actually help you achieve work-life balance by reducing stress and allowing you to focus on what is most important.

In conclusion, achieving work-life balance is a critical aspect of success in the tech industry. Effective time management, self-care, setting boundaries, and asking for help are all important strategies for achieving work-life balance. By prioritizing work-life balance and taking care of yourself, you can prevent burnout, maintain good mental health, and achieve long-term success. Remember, work is an important part of life, but it is not everything. It is essential to take care of yourself and make time for the things that matter most in your personal life.

Techniques for promoting well-being in the workplace, including mindfulness and stress reduction.

In the fast-paced world of IT, workplace stress and burnout are common issues. The demands of the industry can be overwhelming, leaving little time for self-care and relaxation. However, promoting well-being in the workplace is essential to maintaining a healthy and productive workforce. In this chapter, we will explore some techniques for promoting well-being in the workplace, including mindfulness and stress reduction.

Mindfulness is a technique that involves focusing on the present moment and being aware of your thoughts and feelings without judgment. In the workplace, mindfulness can help employees reduce stress and increase focus and productivity. One way to practice mindfulness is through meditation. Taking a few minutes each day to sit quietly and focus on your breath can help you feel more centered and calm. There are also many mindfulness apps available that offer guided meditations and other mindfulness exercises.

Another way to promote well-being in the workplace is through stress reduction techniques. Stress can have a negative impact on physical and mental health, and can also affect job performance. Techniques for reducing stress include exercise, deep breathing, and progressive muscle relaxation. Exercise is a great way to reduce stress and improve overall health. Even a short walk during the workday can help to reduce tension and increase energy levels. Deep breathing is another effective stress reduction technique. Taking slow, deep breaths can help to lower blood pressure and reduce feelings of anxiety. Progressive muscle relaxation involves tensing and then relaxing different muscle groups in the body, which can help to release physical tension and promote relaxation.

In addition to these techniques, there are many other ways to promote well-being in the workplace. One effective strategy is to create a positive work environment. This can be achieved by encouraging open communication, recognizing and celebrating employee accomplishments, and fostering a culture of respect and support. Encouraging employees to take breaks and providing a comfortable and inviting break room can also help to promote well-being in the workplace.

Employers can also promote well-being by offering wellness programs and resources. This can include access to fitness classes, mental health resources, and healthy food options. Many companies also offer employee assistance programs (EAPs), which provide confidential counseling and support for a range of personal and work-related issues.

Finally, it's important for employees to prioritize self-care and to set boundaries between work and personal life. This can include setting aside time for hobbies and leisure activities, spending time with family and friends, and taking vacations. It's also important to disconnect from work emails and messages during non-work hours, and to establish a regular sleep schedule.

In conclusion, promoting well-being in the workplace is essential to maintaining a healthy and productive workforce.

Techniques for promoting well-being include mindfulness, stress reduction, and creating a positive work environment. Employers can also offer wellness programs and resources, and employees can prioritize self-care and set boundaries between work and personal life. By prioritizing well-being in the workplace, employees can reduce stress and burnout, and improve their overall health and job performance.

Chapter Eight

Creativity and Innovation in Tech

An exploration of the importance of creativity and innovation in the tech industry.

The tech industry is constantly evolving, and to stay ahead of the game, innovation and creativity are critical. This is because the industry is highly competitive and demands constant improvement and new ideas. Therefore, innovation and creativity are essential for companies to remain relevant and to offer their customers cutting-edge solutions.

Creativity and innovation can be seen in many aspects of the tech industry, from software development to hardware design, user interface, and experience. Without creativity and innovation, it is challenging to create products that will be well received by the target audience.

Moreover, creativity and innovation go hand in hand with problem-solving skills. The ability to solve complex problems creatively can make a significant difference in the tech industry. Engineers and developers who can identify problems and come up with innovative solutions can create a competitive edge for their company.

Additionally, innovation and creativity can also help companies to streamline their processes and optimize their products. Creative ideas can lead to more efficient processes, which can increase productivity and reduce costs. For example, new software tools or hardware systems that are designed with innovation and creativity in mind can help companies work smarter and not harder.

However, fostering creativity and innovation in the workplace is not always easy. The tech industry is fast-paced and demanding, and employees can become overwhelmed with deadlines, meetings, and workload. Creativity and innovation require time, space, and an open mind. Therefore, promoting a culture that encourages creativity and innovation is vital.

One way to promote creativity and innovation in the workplace is by creating a culture that values experimentation and risk-taking. Employees need to feel safe to take risks and try new things without the fear of failure or reprimand. Failure is often part of the creative process, and allowing employees to fail and learn from their mistakes can lead to breakthrough ideas.

Another way to foster creativity and innovation is by promoting cross-functional collaboration. Different perspectives and experiences can lead to new ideas and solutions that may not have been apparent before. Cross-functional collaboration can also help break down silos and promote knowledge sharing and learning within the organization.

Finally, it is essential to provide employees with the resources and tools they need to be creative and innovative. This includes access to training and development opportunities, tools and equipment, and time to work on personal projects. Encouraging employees to take breaks and recharge is also critical, as creativity and innovation require a fresh mind and a positive attitude.

In conclusion, creativity and innovation are vital for the tech industry to remain competitive and relevant. Companies that foster a culture of creativity and innovation can create a competitive edge and drive their success. It is essential to promote risk-taking, collaboration, and provide the resources and tools employees need to be creative and innovative. By doing so, companies can create products and solutions that exceed customer expectations and stay ahead of the competition.

The role of soft skills, such as curiosity and imagination, in fostering creativity and innovation.

Creativity and innovation are essential for the tech industry, where new ideas and cutting-edge solutions are constantly in demand. However, the role of soft skills, such as curiosity and imagination, in fostering these qualities is often overlooked. In this chapter, we'll explore how soft skills can help drive creativity and innovation in the tech industry.

Curiosity is one of the most critical soft skills that can help fuel creativity and innovation. It involves a genuine interest in learning and exploring new ideas, concepts, and perspectives. Curiosity encourages individuals to ask questions, seek answers, and approach problems with an open mind, all of which are essential for generating innovative solutions.

Another crucial soft skill that supports creativity and innovation is imagination. Imagination involves the ability to visualize and generate new ideas and possibilities, often based on existing concepts or experiences. It allows individuals to think beyond the confines of what already exists and generate novel ideas and solutions.

Empathy is another soft skill that is essential for creativity and innovation in the tech industry. It involves the ability to understand and appreciate the perspectives, needs, and concerns of others. Empathy allows individuals to develop a deep understanding of their customers, clients, and colleagues, which is essential for designing user-friendly products and building effective teams.

Effective communication is also a vital soft skill for creativity and innovation. It involves the ability to express ideas, collaborate with others, and receive feedback effectively. Clear communication allows team members to share their thoughts and perspectives and work together to develop innovative solutions.

Finally, adaptability is another critical soft skill that fosters creativity and innovation in the tech industry. It involves the ability to adjust and respond to changing circumstances, including emerging technologies and evolving market trends. Being adaptable allows individuals and organizations to identify new opportunities and respond quickly and effectively to emerging challenges.

In summary, soft skills play a crucial role in fostering creativity and innovation in the tech industry. Curiosity, imagination, empathy, effective communication, and adaptability are just a few of the soft skills that can help individuals and organizations generate new ideas and solutions. To promote these skills, tech companies must prioritize employee development, offer ongoing training and support, and create a culture that values and rewards creativity and innovation. By doing so, they can help drive the continued growth and success of the industry.

Strategies for developing creativity and innovation skills in the workplace, including brainstorming and experimentation.

Innovation and creativity are vital to the growth and success of any organization, particularly in the fast-paced world of technology. However, creativity is not something that can be forced or simply demanded from employees. It is a skill that needs to be nurtured and encouraged. Below are some strategies for developing creativity and innovation skills in the workplace.

1. Foster a culture of innovation: The first step in developing creativity and innovation skills in the workplace is to create a culture that encourages and supports creativity. Leaders should create an environment where employees feel comfortable sharing their ideas without fear of judgment or ridicule. This can be achieved by setting aside time for brainstorming sessions, providing resources for experimentation, and acknowledging and rewarding employees for their innovative ideas.

2. Encourage collaboration: Collaboration can lead to the exchange of new ideas and perspectives, which can ultimately lead to greater creativity and innovation. Leaders should encourage employees to work in cross-functional teams and provide opportunities for employees to collaborate outside of their typical work teams. This can be achieved through team-building activities, such as group projects or workshops.

3. Provide resources for experimentation: Innovation requires experimentation and risk-taking. Leaders should provide resources for employees to experiment with new ideas and technologies, such as creating a dedicated space for prototyping or providing access to new technologies. This allows employees to explore new ideas without fear of failure or judgment.

4. Embrace diversity: Diversity in the workplace can lead to new ideas and perspectives that may not have been considered otherwise. Leaders should embrace diversity and create a workplace that values and promotes diversity in all its forms, including race, gender, age, and background.

5. Encourage curiosity and continuous learning: Curiosity is an essential component of creativity and innovation. Leaders should encourage employees to be curious and to continuously learn and develop new skills. This can be achieved through professional development programs, mentorship opportunities, and access to educational resources.

6. Use brainstorming techniques: Brainstorming is a powerful tool for generating new ideas and solutions. Leaders should encourage employees to use brainstorming techniques, such as mind mapping or random word association, to explore new ideas and perspectives.

7. Create a safe space for experimentation: Employees need to feel safe to experiment and take risks. Leaders should create a safe space for experimentation where employees are free to try new ideas without fear of

judgment or punishment. This can be achieved by setting clear expectations, providing feedback and support, and celebrating successes and failures alike.

In conclusion, developing creativity and innovation skills in the workplace requires a commitment from leaders to create a culture that fosters innovation, encourages collaboration, and provides resources for experimentation. By embracing diversity, promoting curiosity and continuous learning, using brainstorming techniques, and creating a safe space for experimentation, organizations can cultivate a workforce that is equipped to tackle the challenges of the fast-paced world of technology.

Chapter Nine

Diversity and Inclusion in Tech

An examination of the importance of diversity and inclusion in the tech industry, and the impact it has on business success.

The tech industry has been a driving force in the global economy, and its influence has only grown over the years. However, with this growth comes a responsibility to ensure that diversity and inclusion are at the forefront of the industry's values. The importance of diversity and inclusion in the tech industry cannot be overstated, as it has a significant impact on business success.

One of the most significant benefits of promoting diversity and inclusion in the tech industry is the increase in innovation and creativity. A diverse team brings a wide range of experiences and perspectives to the table, which can lead to new ideas and solutions. This can be particularly beneficial in the fast-paced world of tech, where innovation is key to staying ahead of the competition. A diverse team can also better understand the needs of a diverse customer base, leading to better products and services.

In addition to promoting innovation and creativity, diversity and inclusion in the tech industry can also have a positive impact on company culture. When employees feel valued and included, they are more likely to be engaged and motivated in their work. This can lead to increased productivity, better collaboration, and improved overall performance. A diverse and inclusive workplace can also attract top talent from a wide range of backgrounds, leading to a more skilled and knowledgeable workforce.

Another important reason for promoting diversity and inclusion in the tech industry is the ethical responsibility that comes with having such a significant impact on society. Technology is shaping the way we live, work, and interact with each other, and it is essential that the industry reflects the diversity of the people it serves. The tech industry has a responsibility to ensure that its products and services are accessible and inclusive for all, regardless of their race, gender, or background.

To promote diversity and inclusion in the tech industry, companies can take a variety of actions. One of the most critical steps is to create a welcoming and inclusive culture. This can be done by fostering an environment of respect and open communication, where everyone feels valued and heard. Companies can also implement diversity and inclusion training programs, to help employees better understand and appreciate different perspectives and experiences.

Another strategy for promoting diversity and inclusion in the tech industry is to actively recruit a diverse workforce. This can be done by partnering with organizations that support underrepresented groups, such as women and minorities. Companies can also review their hiring practices to ensure that they are inclusive and unbiased.

Cross-cultural communication is another crucial aspect of promoting diversity and inclusion in the tech industry. Effective communication is essential for building strong relationships and collaborating effectively with people from diverse backgrounds. Companies can implement training programs that focus on improving cross-cultural communication skills, such as active listening and empathy.

In conclusion, the importance of diversity and inclusion in the tech industry cannot be overstated. It has a significant impact on innovation, company culture, and ethical responsibility. By promoting diversity and inclusion, companies can create a more innovative, engaged, and skilled workforce, while also ensuring that their products and services are accessible and inclusive for all. Strategies such as creating a welcoming and inclusive culture, actively recruiting a diverse workforce, and improving cross-cultural communication skills can help companies achieve these goals.

Strategies for promoting diversity and inclusion in the workplace, including creating a welcoming and inclusive culture.

Diversity and inclusion are critical components of a successful workplace culture. Not only do they help to create a sense of belonging for all employees, but they also lead to greater creativity, innovation, and collaboration. In the tech industry, where innovation is king, creating a diverse and inclusive culture is especially important. Here are some strategies for promoting diversity and inclusion in the workplace, including creating a welcoming and inclusive culture.

1. Encourage open communication: One of the most important things you can do to create a welcoming and inclusive culture is to encourage open communication among your employees. This means creating an environment where everyone feels comfortable sharing their ideas, opinions, and experiences. Encourage your team to speak up, and make sure they know that their voices are being heard and valued.

2. Provide training: Provide training and workshops on diversity, inclusion, and cultural competence. This can help your employees become more aware of their own biases and become more culturally sensitive. You can also provide training on how to communicate effectively with people from different cultures.

3. Create a diversity and inclusion task force: Create a task force dedicated to promoting diversity and inclusion in the workplace. This group can help to identify areas where your company can improve and develop strategies for promoting a more inclusive culture. Make sure this task force includes employees from different backgrounds and levels of the organization.

4. Celebrate diversity: Celebrate the diversity of your team and your customers. Recognize and celebrate holidays and cultural events that are important to your employees. This can help to create a sense of belonging and make everyone feel included.

5. Make diversity and inclusion part of your company's values: Make sure that diversity and inclusion are part of your company's core values. This can help to ensure that these principles are integrated into everything your company does, from hiring to product development.

6. Hire for diversity: Make sure that your hiring process is designed to attract a diverse range of candidates. This means posting job openings in a variety of places and making sure your job descriptions are inclusive. You can also partner with organizations that focus on diversity and inclusion to help you find diverse candidates.

7. Create mentorship and networking opportunities: Create mentorship and networking opportunities for employees from underrepresented groups. This can help to create a sense of community and provide support for employees who may feel isolated or marginalized.

8. Conduct diversity audits: Conduct regular diversity audits to assess your company's progress in promoting diversity and inclusion. This can help you identify areas where you need to improve and develop strategies for making meaningful changes.

Creating a diverse and inclusive culture is not easy, and it takes time and effort. However, the benefits of doing so are significant, including greater creativity, innovation, and collaboration. By following these strategies, you can help to create a workplace culture that celebrates diversity and promotes inclusion.

Techniques for improving cross-cultural communication and working effectively in diverse teams.

In today's globalized world, it is increasingly common to find diverse teams in the workplace. This diversity can bring many benefits, but it can also present challenges, particularly when it comes to cross-cultural communication. To ensure that everyone in a diverse team feels heard, understood, and valued, it is essential to develop effective cross-cultural communication skills. Here are some techniques that can help:

1. Listen actively and with an open mind. Active listening involves paying close attention to what someone is

saying and trying to understand their perspective. In a diverse team, it is essential to listen actively to colleagues from different backgrounds to avoid misunderstandings and miscommunication.

2. Avoid making assumptions. We all have our biases and preconceptions, but it is important to recognize them and avoid making assumptions about people based on their cultural background. Instead, take the time to learn about your colleagues' cultures and be open to different ways of thinking and working.

3. Clarify your understanding. To ensure that you have understood someone correctly, it can be helpful to repeat what they have said in your own words or ask them to clarify if you are unsure. This can prevent misunderstandings and help to build trust and respect.

4. Be aware of nonverbal communication. In some cultures, nonverbal cues such as facial expressions, gestures, and body language can carry more meaning than words. It is important to be aware of these cues and to be sensitive to cultural differences in nonverbal communication.

5. Use simple and clear language. When communicating with colleagues who are not fluent in your language, it can be helpful to use simple and clear language, avoid jargon and technical terms, and to speak slowly and clearly.

6. Be respectful of different communication styles. Different cultures have different communication styles, and it is important to be respectful of these differences.

For example, some cultures may value indirect communication or may avoid confrontation. Being aware of these differences can help to avoid misunderstandings and promote effective communication.

7. Build relationships with colleagues from diverse backgrounds. To work effectively in a diverse team, it is essential to build relationships and to develop trust and mutual respect. This can involve learning about your colleagues' cultures, interests, and backgrounds, and finding common ground.

8. Be flexible and adaptable. Working in a diverse team requires flexibility and adaptability. This may mean being open to new ideas and ways of working, and being willing to adjust your communication style to suit the needs of your colleagues.

9. Seek feedback and be open to constructive criticism. To improve your cross-cultural communication skills, it can be helpful to seek feedback from colleagues from different backgrounds and to be open to constructive criticism. This can help you to identify areas for improvement and to develop more effective communication strategies.

In conclusion, effective cross-cultural communication is essential for working effectively in diverse teams. By listening actively, avoiding assumptions, being aware of nonverbal communication, using simple and clear language, being respectful of different communication styles, building relationships, being flexible and adaptable, seeking feedback, and being open to constructive criticism, you can develop the skills you need to communicate effectively with colleagues from diverse backgrounds. By promoting diversity and inclusion in the workplace, we can create a more innovative, productive, and harmonious work environment.

Conclusions

In today's fast-paced world of technology, success is no longer just about having technical expertise. To thrive in the industry, IT professionals must also have strong soft skills, such as emotional intelligence, communication, collaboration, leadership, conflict resolution, work-life balance, creativity and innovation, and diversity and inclusion. These skills are essential for building relationships, navigating complex work environments, and driving innovation.

Emotional intelligence, for example, is critical for understanding and managing one's own emotions, as well as those of others. Effective communication skills are also essential, as they enable IT professionals to express ideas clearly and work effectively with others. Collaboration and teamwork are key for ensuring that projects are completed on time and to a high standard, while leadership and management skills are essential for motivating and guiding teams.

Conflict resolution skills are critical for dealing with disputes that can arise in the tech industry, and work-life balance and well-being are important for preventing burnout and maintaining productivity. Creativity and innovation skills are also crucial for driving the development of new products and services, while diversity and inclusion are essential for creating a welcoming and inclusive workplace.

To develop these skills, IT professionals can take various steps, such as attending training and development programs, seeking feedback from colleagues, and practicing mindfulness and stress reduction techniques. They can also use strategies such as time management and self-care to achieve work-life balance, and techniques such as brainstorming and experimentation to promote creativity and innovation. Finally, they can work to create a welcoming and inclusive culture, through initiatives such as employee resource groups and diversity training programs.

Overall, the key takeaway from this book is that success in the tech industry is no longer just about technical expertise. Soft skills are now essential for building relationships, driving innovation, and creating a positive work environment. By developing these skills, IT professionals can position themselves for success in their careers, and help their organizations stay ahead in a constantly evolving industry.

Final thoughts on the importance of soft skills in IT, and why they should be prioritized.

In conclusion, soft skills are essential for success in the fast-paced world of information technology. While technical skills are undoubtedly important, they are no longer sufficient on their own. Employers are increasingly recognizing the value of soft skills and the role they play in creating a positive workplace culture and driving business success.

The ability to communicate effectively, collaborate with others, and think creatively are all crucial components of success in IT. Emotional intelligence and conflict resolution skills are equally important in today's diverse and dynamic workplaces.

Moreover, promoting work-life balance, prioritizing employee well-being, and fostering an inclusive workplace culture are also critical factors in promoting a positive work environment and driving innovation.

As the tech industry continues to evolve and become more competitive, the need for soft skills will only continue to grow. Employers must recognize the importance of prioritizing the development of soft skills in their employees to ensure the continued success of their business.

For IT professionals, investing in the development of soft skills will not only help them advance in their careers, but it will also help them to stand out in a crowded job market.

In short, soft skills are no longer a nice-to-have in the world of IT - they are a must-have. By prioritizing the development of these skills, both employers and employees can ensure long-term success and thrive in the rapidly evolving tech industry.

A call to action for IT professionals to continue developing their soft skills for success in their careers.

As the world becomes increasingly digital, the demand for skilled IT professionals continues to grow. While technical skills are important in this field, it's equally important to remember the significance of soft skills. These skills allow professionals to work well in teams, communicate effectively with colleagues and clients, and problem-solve in a dynamic environment. It's crucial that IT professionals continue to prioritize the development of their soft skills, as they will be key to their success in the industry.

Therefore, it is time to take action and actively work on improving your soft skills. Seek out opportunities to practice your communication, collaboration, and leadership skills, both in and outside of work. Consider attending workshops or seminars on topics such as emotional intelligence, active listening, and conflict resolution. Take advantage of training programs and courses offered by your employer, or seek out online resources to further develop your soft skills.

Furthermore, it's important to prioritize diversity and inclusion in the workplace. Actively work to create a welcoming and inclusive culture, and strive to understand and appreciate the unique perspectives and experiences of your colleagues. Seek out opportunities to learn about different cultures and backgrounds, and be open to feedback and constructive criticism.

In summary, the IT industry is constantly evolving, and the demand for soft skills is increasing. It's essential for IT professionals to prioritize the development of these skills, as they will be key to their success in the industry. By taking action and actively working on improving their soft skills, IT professionals can contribute to a more collaborative and inclusive work environment, ultimately leading to greater success for themselves and their organizations.

Printed in Great Britain
by Amazon